Insights and wisdoms..

Flash or flows of insights should know the ways of morals.

Human insights are quite an inventive thing.

Life needs penetrating insights.

What priorities are peoples one, two, three estates?

Peoples' regards but PINKO esteems are very proud.

Who wants for justices?

Who seek their happiness?

What insights are human natures?

Who is selfish and love to make use the other all?

Try to be wise and try to make senses always.

Try to know more and learn more that gain by thinking are wisdoms coming.

Things such as ideas or a fact that is full of values and if you can know as your wisdoms

Wisdoms are the under taking about our facts and do a lot design and program.

Programs are do with good designs of human styles for

functions of life.

---------------Cheung Shun Sang=Cauchy3----------------

    Some ways of life….

Who motive from the places outside and care a lot of psychologies.

Who motive from the inner may search fir a heart of gold,

Fields that cover perceptions, motivations, emotions, cognitions have physical ways that affected by our brains or nervous.

For brains and claim that true are always ideas and sexy libido.

Express your feeling so the others could know you.

Life has moods and there should be notions that good for morals beside self interests and self to something ends. .

Ways of morals made up by ways of good or bad

That society says.

Made your notions to do the best and so morally are good colors of life.

Notions can be good.

Notions could be bad.

Notional things can idealize by harnesses that collar self.

Notional things can be something real when you try.

But mass psychology or principal and even to most are martyr deaths with wails or henchman easy groans

--------------Cheung Shun Sang=CXauchy3----------------- .
,

    Better..

Cultures run down and pass to men by speeches or showing of men.

Sometimes chanted and sung.

Folktales, quotations, magic spells are different types of instructions or recollections about our society and cultures passing on.

Something optimists encourage our worlds.

But pessimists make us taking care about what happens.

For psychologies if you see a heart that draw on wall on your street if you try to think that it i s loves then you are optimists.

On the other hand if you are pessimists you say with sure with that it is graffiti or tagging.

But with marks also graffiti on walls of streets that could human lions pissing.

That marks and dirty paints show that who closely in charge of that turfs or grounds by those gangs and we should know now.

What superpowers are you looking as SHAMAN or angels from Christ?

As see in futures are big chances then this fancies on ways bring a man that invent things in futures.

If you think that you have special power.

Then only the foods or stuffs of thoughts then you begin

to know your selves as dreams or fantasy.

Jump out of your boundary if you can and if you know yourselves.

---------------Cheung Shun Sang=Cauchy3----------------

    Human cannibalism….

Is human cannibalism…

Certain men capture and consume the moneys and labor forces of the poor,.

Are there menu for catechism that fetch the meaning of faith, hopes and charity.

But what make our world get quite a lot of crony capitalizations.

Are there themes to good as christen socialism.

They try to mingle the aims of socialism that would combine with religion ethics.

Just keep hands to hands without fighting to help the

poor and lower classes.

But when can we buy our bursting themes.

Are we putsch for a better china but we cannot.

----------------Cheung Shun Sang=Cauchy3--------

Regulated…

Moods control the speed of times sucking.

Happy with lucks but calm in life are flexible life.

Actual life is wired oranges that skew.

Smooth or acid are carrots or sticks.

Wooden plums or wooden nickels are so trickery.

Caught short is ways of us to play the water sports with china tyrants of course we active and give and wet them under the praise of many peoples.

CAUSATIONISTS all must be relate theme that coherence or on the other ways they are being punished.

Some can sum up that means and both must conjoined as cabal then they are evil CAUSATIONISTS.

There may also regularity analysis, counterfactual analysis and probability analysis.

Those above are scientific philosophy themes of life.

Are there always sexes after loves between two legal one.

Are there suckers as there are poets?

He may be SUCKLING SIR JOHN the poet.

Weight our earth and there are gravitational forces.

Now do you believe to science?

But as you sow so will you reap.

I might like to give my after kisses or even HICKIE.

Who to be worthy of the names of gods and as there are china tyrant leaders CAUDILLISMO.

---------------Cheung Shun Sang=Cauchy3---------

Bad...

Wail and bad are dictated country

No gods embodied but morals cares that are good and must.

Bones are scraping to rural dogs.

Witticisms know the worlds of dogs and bones.

Ok you are right and you on top.

Bottom men are kowtow men.

Codes of laws are outcomes just as double deals.

True liberties all are just daydreams.

No drugs but instant ZEN.

Meditate a lot calmly and think about the happy and sad theme of life.

Govern fall in token ways.

Go down to me and no more tokenism.

Dark clouds and bad smokes are whelming.

Citizen rights are feathers of chick.

High are costs are seizing our rights.

Who confine their body by refraining souls?

Who demoralize the china evil troops?

Many maniples are sixty nine as PICES sexual life.

Many china leaders henchman go down on their leaders as sexes of disciples.

Who kill their peoples and vanish the peaceful protest of their pupils in something non-fair s.

Manic depressive all are leaders bipolar so fierce or so shame.

All are obsessive compulsive behavioral for some.

China leaders and army could kill the innocents.

Nothing self-blame but ways of dementia insanity and premature is china leaders' madness.

The anxiety of people is always access.

Negative born are dictated forces.

There are governing acute durations.

Very sharp and fierce and forceful are that.

Should over bearing and bossy classes have classifications but take their history books that written but follow their tyrants' ways that juggled for some history.

No china chairman are most devolve their powers and army Ranks easily.

Unless for those decisions from their single big along political party the commie party.

Privilege and control forces are harsh and tight.

Words and essays justify the true history must needed.

We are hungry for human rights.

We are hungry for democracy..

No mannerisms nervous are good so even being oppressed we had to keep calm.

We are not being hypnotized but we all hate the china tyranny.

Books are cooked and jades are burnt.

----------------Cheung Shun Sang=Cauchy3-------------

MANO-A-MANO....

Heavily guarded ranges are Taiwan uphold.

However no MANO-A-MANO but it is peace that work.

Our valiant wills raise as spirits are natural high.

To aim high and quell the vices and life is square deals is good.

Hold our grounds and Taiwan must stand strong with freedoms.

Try our best to fight for right.

With weapons plays it is counter for vices.

All dagger drawn but nowadays we use cannons and missiles.

Cutthroats diligent have sophisticate works.

Loves to loves and peace will still need the even and justices.

Fight for right the alternative counters are also only fight for rights.

---------------Cheung Shun Sang=Cauchy3------------

Pelting….

Missiles pelting broke the mountains.

Patriot missiles are good and America balances the trend of forces around our earth.

America landscapes are very important around the earth.

Army zones and weapons are set and fix all around.

But I am Chinese.

Pleader cases are well speak as about as dreams.

Mirror dusts are minds that should clear.

OPU DEI is ideas of dreams.

Some elongated cells will like the feel of dreams.

Dreams are phantom ways but easy for sleep.

Dirty sleepy needed as nurses of life.

Sleep and dreams will infuse our pillows loves.

Lean and foolish all are dreams that repressed from struggling living.

Pelting loves are sleeps are dreams that filled or modify our desires.

Pelt to turn our coats and not so cold or chill that is pelting.

Good polishers' opinions poll my pelting.

Human life is god possessory so then for pelting we are quite innocent.

However we have our free wills so our very life endure the cruel swears or oaths as dues and as our responsibility.

Now tiger jumps so near our cannons and our cannons may pelt.

What I mean only the life of soldiers always so quick like smart like the fierce tigers or cannon but I am only a humble poet.

Principles are definitely good so there are pelting for your behave or ways.

Life resonances are all as hitting or pelting ways with burst files.

Wayward loves are always pelting and quarreling.

------Cheung Shun Sang=Cauchy3-----------

Gods that hate..

Gods are hauled on ground and kisses become affections.

Who afford no credits after the after math that gods may loves and god may sexes.

Roll my cards and loves can be taken as half to half before whole at ends.

Sun or moon and golden bras to read and makes our senses.

Sun or moon are golden flames are sink and swim of common life.

See the exploited us copies of histories.

True obey is very serious god disciples.

That is why china tyrants pretend that they are very tops and even they are china DEMI GODS.

Hollow hearts have nothing honor.

Careful child can be very very nice child.

Hoof and kick is stamp on ways.

Foot no laws and should stamped if there are

demonstrations.

We are old we are live in life that with times and ages that earn.

Life and death is sometimes seem to control by fates.

Take the apple for fruit of EDEN but gods have treaties.

Gymnasts stand on trapeze.

Gods stand and walk on sea surfaces.

Can you fix what is true and what is false.

Fetus cannot birth when shed.

Gods cannot birth without dirty sexes.

Queen has wombs and Tummy but goddess have spells in vain.

EINSTERRN is free and fair for death.

By EINSTERN our worlds are much better.

AS china tyrant leaders they al dictated and edited that as control most of us and there we obey with our lame instincts.

Who handle the birth of gods and who haul our gods to courts?

Religions stress on loves as fulfill life then what about us.

-----------------Cheung Shun Sang=Cauchy3--------------

How and now…..

Pleasures are normally gathers of comforts but abnormally they are pains.

Approval to well orders social ways are means of life.

Conquests are bonus is merit cases.

But made us self aware are social conscience sometimes.

Life attributes are health and high of egos.

China tyrants wastages can be peoples fair life.

Life engenders love.

Clear have classic conflict.

Just let us work without knowing the reasons that is china tyranny.

China forcers and ill and bad intentions engrain much.

What is fair and most all are fair deaths?

What exert influences and hold it strong.

Juggle histories all should appeal by upright ways and trim.

China tyrants superiority complexes want to look down upon many.

Straight mean if what I wish them to correct their life.

But what they redeemed is null and void.

Who can constitute against by simple means?

Let our life so right as there are cause and effects as what it may be.

---------------Cheung Shun Sang=Cauchy3 ----------------

That…

What is that but that is that.

AS common one we had to agree the china tyrants team

for wills.

Closely guarded are visible laws.

What exceptions are leaders' bossy wills.

POPOLO ways are living fairs.

Why do we win the ideas but the china cruel bad laws win us.

All are touching if you own a lots of possessions or even very political powers.

All are retributions from peoples if there are worlds and social justices.

Such as publicize are show hands that show your cards.

Ultra-lights know by forms of weaves.

Peoples' hearts are known by deeds and manners.

Trends and declines are normal fates.

What outcome would be evils?

China tyrants mean to use forces to govern normal coming and going.

Laws have details but not abridges.

Men of four letters leading us are tyrants.

Of courses there are china real politics that make their peoples real to suffer.

What to weight their own are china tyrants are self important to end.

-------------Cheung Shun sang=Cauchy3-------------

    Loves on way,.

Loves on ways and there are gentle manners.

Soft and sweet as dreams are loving partners.

Grand and smarts are martyr loves.

Tyranny chins evil party cults are wrong.

Let us on and reactions come from us.

Life can made many unequal rational.

Protests with moral asking are better than dresses parade.

Worlds as earth are human continuum.

There must have true loves to live on.

A clinching argument may be convoluted with sounds

but what we need are justices and also loves.

However facts and cause and effects may be nothing easy.

Break your golden cuffs and work for truths and justices and loves.

Do and praise our intentions for loves.

Take humane and care our human life.

China tyrants talks are humanity justices and moral but there are something very bad in all their inner characters that hide under hides.

Humanity would come if there are loves and kindness.

Are you are pure?

Are you are be good with humane and loves.

China tyrants' backgrounds have superiority complexes.

What super egos are needy needs?

When curtains of life fall then all will loss , but would there are still smiles in graves.

----------------Cheung Shun Sang=Cauchy3--------------

Instruments...

Pets are toys.

China common peoples are china leaders' instruments.

Instruments china peoples when bold and dare they test and follow tyrant leaders wills.

Machiavellian ways are planning instruments are tricks.

Machiavellian tricks are also instrument so call and fix.

They have instruments that lie and despotic.

What destabilize are so clean and right and fair. It is only nemesis.

What made the worlds that swim or sink?

What destiny is moral comes?

What a theme are as china tyrants repress the feeling of shame and sins.

What detached laws is nothing fair.

Life detachedly made but still is instruments.

----------Cheung Shun Sang=Cauchy3----------------

Repress....

Yes china tyrants like the XI JINPING teams are human being.

But they repress their shameful feels and guilty sense so they may be abnormal.

AS many bad themes then their mental brains are so dull or maniac in bipolar moods then they are sick.

One day they might become mad or crazy says like to run amuck.

Negative forces that hide or repressed just like latent evil forces are trends for access schizophrenia.

As a matter of facts our inside worlds need morals.

But most of all the china leaders are hypocrites.

Better life and better mental health is ideological.

What are good fettles?

It is body mind that sound.

-------------Cheung Shun Sang=cauchy3-------------

Some gods...

Can wills and feels and senses discover ouir god and gods in our minds are normal?

Can reasons without science prove and that is also nothing axioms can make us believe our worlds can give us god or gods.

Deism ways can take for favors and some noble persons are deism disciples.

Deism stresses on that reason that must be a god to create our world.

Going on natural means as universal rules and orders are gods wills.

So as in followers then we must to live under sit by natures normal orders.

Sensations are SENSIBILIAS.

Minds and matters can be good or bad.

Gods and worlds are beliefs but they are also something objective real.

No gods in reality but there are gods in beliefs only.

In normal life our defense mechanisms or our senses of safes or dangers may made us have our foolish reasons to believe to gods.

May be it is impulses or emotions that caused by sadness or other mental weakness so that make believe that we need a figures gods as tokens,

------------Cheung Shun Sang=Cauchy3-----------

www.ingramcontent.com/pod-product-compliance
Lightning Source LLC
Chambersburg PA
CBHW070736180526
45167CB00004B/1777